The Progression of Ministry

By

PHILLIP RICH

EKKLISIA PROPHETIC APOSTOLIC MINISTRIES, INC.

PUBLISHED BY EKKLISIA MINISTRIES, INC
Copyright 2005 A. D.

All rights reserved under International Copyright law. No part of this publication may be reproduced, stored in a retrieval system, or transmitted, in whole or in part, in any form or by any means, electronic, mechanical, photocopying, recording or otherwise, without the prior express consent of the publisher. All scripture is the Kings James Version unless otherwise stated. All rights reserved.

Take note that the name satan is not capitalized. We choose not to acknowledge him, even to the point of violating grammatical rules.

Table of Contents

Anointed For Ministry 1

Approved For Ministry 14

Appointed For Ministry 34

ANOINTED FOR MINISTRY

God has called all of us. There isn't anyone who is not called into the ministry. If you are a born again child of God, if you are a servant of the Lord, then you are saved and called into a ministry. Those called to the five-fold ministry are called to equip the saints to do the work of the ministry.

There are some things we don't understand about the anointing. We know God anoints but we don't understand that God anoints for a reason. Many times the anointing will come as a reward for something you have come through.

We are going to look at when the anointing came to Jesus and how that anointing came on His life. There are some things we didn't know but they have been in the Word all along. About the time we think we know everything about something, the Holy Ghost comes along and lets us know we don't know anything yet. He brings progressive, ongoing revelation. There is no end to the revelation that God can bring. That is what is so exciting about being with the Father, Jesus and the Holy Ghost for all eternity. There will be no end to revelation. God will constantly be revealing Himself every moment, every second of eternity. He will thrill us every moment with revelation.

You may think you are going to know it all in heaven but there is not a scripture that tells us that. That is what religion has taught us. It is not a once you get there you will know it all situation. The Bible says we will know as we are known. That simply means we are going to know each other not that we are going to know everything. We are going to tap into the mind of Christ but He is going to be unveiling, teaching, revealing.

The Holy Ghost is the revealer and He will not stop being the revealer in eternity. He will not quit being the revealer when we reach heaven. He is a teacher. He will not quit just because we get to heaven. What is so awesome about it is that He is all of these things to us right now. We have the ability to enter whatever is revealed to us. With every revelation comes an impartation to receive the manifestation. If you can get that in your heart, excitement will begin to build.

2 Corinthians 3:5-6; *"Not that we are sufficient of ourselves to think any thing as of ourselves; but our sufficiency is of God; Who also hath made us able ministers of the new testament; not of the letter, but of the spirit: for the letter killeth, but the spirit giveth life."*

All of us are ministers of the new covenant, of the New Testament but some are called as five-fold ministers who train other ministers. There is a place for all of us to have a ministry. We all have a calling. We all have a congregation. For some our family is our congregation. Our neighbors, the people we work with are our congregation. Everybody has a ministry and everybody has a congregation. The five-fold ministry is to equip you to do the stuff. They are to impart into you, stir you and release into you that which is necessary for you to fulfill your ministry in the earth.

Acts 10:38 tells us how God anointed Jesus of Nazareth with the Holy Ghost and with power. He went about doing good and healing all those who were oppressed of the devil for God was with Him. God is the one who anoints. The anointing doesn't come from man. God can use a man to release it on someone, but the originator of the anointing is God. Just like He is the author and finisher of our faith, He is also the author of the anointing. It comes from Him.

God doesn't just put the anointing on everybody but everyone can acquire it. There are certain qualifying criteria to be met.

Just because I may feel excited or exuberant or because I may feel some anointing doesn't mean I am anointed. The anointing is not a feeling, though you can feel it. It is ability. My wife is not a feeling. She is a person. But she can give me a hug and a kiss and I will feel it down to my toes.

The Holy Ghost is the person who anoints. God releases the anointing through the Spirit of God. We have heard the anointing described as the yoke-destroying, burden-removing power of God. The anointing is God's ability released into the lives of humans so that humans can do God's work effectively in the earth with positive results.

You are not really anointed until somebody else knows you are anointed. You are not anointed because you know you are. The anointing is not what I feel upon me. I do feel it when I am anointed but it is not for me to feel. It is for someone else to feel, for someone else's life to be touched, for someone else's life to be changed. God anoints me to minister to others. God anoints me to touch the lives of others, anoints you to touch the lives of others. The anointing is there to touch somebody else to bring about positive change in their life for Jesus Christ.

THE PROGRESSION

I have heard people teach on how God anoints people, how powerful the anointing is, how it changes lives, how wonderful it is. We need to hear that. But I have never heard teaching on how the anointing comes. Some will say you need to fast, pray and wait on God. Yes and no. That is not really the progression in the scripture. Let me show you how Jesus got it. If you can see how Jesus got it then you will know how you can get it. We know He was anointed. We know He is still anointed.

We are going to look at the progression of the anointing in the life of Jesus because He came to the place where He qualified for it. He was destined to be the Christ – the Anointed One and His anointing. But I hope you understand He wasn't that from birth. Positionally He was, but not experientially, until He qualified to step into it.

Luke 3:21-22; *"Now when all the people were baptized, it came to pass, that Jesus also being baptized, and praying, the heaven was opened, And the Holy Ghost descended in a bodily shape like a dove upon him, and a voice came from heaven, which said, Thou art my beloved Son; in thee I am well pleased."*

This scripture does not say the Holy Ghost is a dove. He descended in a bodily shape *like* a dove. The Holy Ghost is not a bird any more than Jesus is a furry creature called a lamb. Yet, He is the lamb that was slain. The Holy Ghost looks just like Jesus. The Trinity looks like one another.

The disciples asked Jesus to show them the Father. Jesus answered by asking them if they had been with Him so long that they did not know that when they saw Him, they saw the Father.[1] Jesus was saying He looks just like the Father and the Father just like Him. Genesis 1 says **"God said, Let us make man in our image, after our likeness."** That was the Trinity (Father, Son, and Holy Ghost) talking to one another. They were saying they wanted to make man to look just like themselves. We do not look like birds or lambs and the Trinity doesn't either.

How many of you have heard people say they had a visitation of Jesus where He just walked into the room and talked to them? Jesus is seated at the right hand of the Father to make intercession for us. He is not coming back till later. In His spirit body form He is in heaven, not here. Yet, when someone says they saw Jesus walk into their room, sit down and talk to them were they lying to us? No. The Holy Ghost will walk into somebody's room and look just like Jesus. The Holy Ghost was sent by Jesus because He was going to go away. If Jesus did not go away, the Comforter would not come. On the Day of Pentecost He arrived. He looks just like Jesus because the Holy Ghost is a person, not just an invisible cloud. However, the Holy Spirit does not speak of Himself. He represents Jesus. He testifies of Jesus.[2]

We know that Jesus was baptized by the Holy Ghost when the Holy Ghost came upon Him. The meaning of those words *"came upon"* is the same as found in Acts 2:1-4.

Acts 2:1-4; *"And when the day of Pentecost was fully come, they were all with one accord in one place. And suddenly there came a sound from heaven as of a rushing mighty wind, and it filled all the house where they were sitting. And there*

---

[1] John 14:9
[2] John chapters 14-16

appeared unto them cloven tongues like as of fire, and it sat upon each of them. And they were all filled with the Holy Ghost, and began to speak with other tongues, as the Spirit gave them utterance."

We know this *"coming upon"* as the baptism of the Holy Spirit.

Before the Holy Ghost comes in, He comes upon. He will descend upon you in a visitation looking for a habitation. He is visiting to see if He can stay, to see if the dwelling place has the accommodations He likes. We can take this kind of visitation all the way back to Noah's ark. It had rained and rained and they were waiting for the waters to go down. Along the way they sent a dove out. The dove could find no resting place. He went on a visitation but couldn't find a habitation. Later the dove was sent out again on a visitation but this time he didn't return. He had found a habitation.

The Holy Ghost may start coming upon you but He may not stay or reside. There are a lot of Christians who have a visitation of the Spirit but not the habitation. There are churches that have revival once a year and the Holy Spirit will come visit. He is not visiting because He is pleased but to see if He can stay. Most of the time He doesn't stay but will come back the next year. Why does He keep coming back? The desire of the heart of God is for His Spirit to find habitation. He will send His Spirit out. The eyes of the Lord run to and fro throughout the whole earth to show Himself strong on the behalf of those whose heart are mature, perfect before Him.[3] He is looking for a heart that is right.

---

[3] 2 Chronicles 16:9

There are a lot of people who feel the anointing upon them but there is nothing in them flowing out.

Elijah went to see Elisha because God told him to anoint a prophet in his place. So he went to see Elisha and threw his mantle over his shoulders. He just let the mantle touch him so that Elisha could feel it. He felt the anointing but it didn't mean he was anointed yet. Just because you have a little feeling, a little spring in your step doesn't mean you are anointed yet. Elisha had to go after it. He had to kill the oxen. He had to go after the man of God.

Luke 4:1; *"And Jesus being full of the Holy Ghost returned from Jordan, and was led by the Spirit into the wilderness,"*

You can't be full of the Holy Ghost unless the Holy Ghost has come within. First, He came *upon*, then He came *within* Jesus and filled Him. When Jesus was baptized, the Word doesn't say He was anointed. When He was filled, it didn't say He was anointed. He was led by the Spirit into the wilderness but still not anointed. There was a progression to coming into the anointing.

The Holy Ghost took Jesus into a wilderness experience. It didn't say He had sinned. It didn't say He messed up or that He could take authority over the wilderness and never have to go through it. It said that He was baptized by the Holy Ghost, filled with the Holy Ghost and led by the Holy Ghost. The Holy Ghost was going to lead Him into a wilderness, not to destroy Him, but to equip Him. He was going to get something out of that, understand some things, and receive some things in the wilderness. He was going to come out on the other side with something He didn't have when He went in.

Jesus was tempted forty days by the devil. I am not going to go into the temptations but I believe that all ministers, before they are released into the fullness of all that God has for them, will hit a place in the spirit where the enemy will lay the cards out on the table.

Jesus used revelation knowledge of the Word of God to defeat the devil in the temptations. He did not use the logos word but the rhema word.

Luke 4:13-14; *"And when the devil had ended all the temptation, he departed from him for a season. And Jesus returned in the power of the Spirit into Galilee: and there went out a fame of him through all the region round about."*

All ready there are beginning to be signs of something. Something He didn't have when He went into the wilderness. He returned and began to operate in the power of the Spirit. This is not the full-fledged anointing yet, but it is the start of it.

Luke 4:15-21; *"And he taught in their synagogues, being glorified of all. And he came to Nazareth, where he had been brought up: and, as his custom was, he went into the synagogue on the sabbath day, and stood up for to read. And there was delivered unto him the book of the prophet Esaias. And when he had opened the book, he found the place where it was written, The Spirit of the Lord is upon me, because he hath anointed me to preach* [to proclaim it] *the gospel to the poor; he hath sent me to heal the brokenhearted, to preach* [to prophesy] *deliverance to the captives, and recovering of sight to the blind, to set at liberty them that are bruised, To preach* [to prophesy] *the acceptable year of the Lord. And he closed the book, and he gave it again to the minister, and sat down. And the eyes of all them that were in the synagogue were* *fastened on him. And he began to say unto them, <u>This day</u> is this scripture fulfilled in your ears."*

When He finished reading about the anointing and what Isaiah had to say about it, He sat down in a chair called the Messiah's chair. No one was allowed to sit in that chair because it was for the Messiah to sit in when He came. Jesus was saying He was the Messiah. Then He said, **"This day is this scripture fulfilled in your ears."** The moment He sat down, He said He was anointed.

On what day did He get anointed? This day – not yesterday. It wasn't when He was baptized by the Holy Ghost. It wasn't when He was filled with the Holy Ghost. It wasn't when He was led by the Holy Ghost into the wilderness. It wasn't when He was tempted of the devil. It wasn't when He was out in the wilderness battling. It wasn't even when He returned, even though there was something different about Him. He had some power He didn't have before. That was the start of it.

He walked into the synagogue and they handed Him the scroll of Isaiah. He opened up the scroll to the right place. A much more difficult task than finding a scripture today. Scrolls did not have chapter headings, numbers or verses. He read the passage, closed the scroll, sat down and said to them, **"This day is this scripture fulfilled in your ears."**

Let me share a secret with you. Something happens when I walk through a hard place, get hold of the Word of God and stand against the devil. On the other side of the attack an anointing is there waiting for me that I did not have before. I don't know of very many people who have not faced something. You can walk through it and say, *"It is written…it is written. I rebuke you devil in the name of Jesus. I command you to back off. I command you to loose. I command you to leave.*" And we stand our ground. Having done all we can, we stand with our loins gird about with truth. We put on the whole armor of God that we may be able to stand against the wiles of the devil.[4]

What do you think the armor of God is for? There is a battle going on and God gives you His armor. It is called the armor of God. Not your armor or my armor. God says to use His armor, to put on the whole armor of God. When you do, you will be able to stand against the wiles of the devil. After you have stood, he will leave you. When he leaves you, get ready. There is an anointing you did not have before that will settle on the top of you.

In my life I have fought tumors, growth and cancers. I fought them with the Word, with faith, with rebuking, and by standing against them. I stood until the devil had to back off. God is gracious and His Word works. You will find out in the midst of the battle how powerful your God really is. It is not by works of righteousness that I have done but His mercy. I simply used His armor and have seen tumors and growths disappear in my own body. Ever since then when I start talking about tumors and growth the anointing comes. People have testified everywhere I go about having tumors and growths disappear in their bodies just sitting in the service listening. Where did I get that anointing? By fighting against tumors and growths. Have you ever seen somebody get a healing? Have you then seen that same person release healing to somebody else? Have you ever seen somebody set free from alcohol or drugs? They have the anointing to set somebody else free.

---

[4] Ephesians 6:11-15

ANOINTINGS

Let me show you how it works. Jesus understood it, so He worked this principle over and over.

Philippians 2:5-11; *"Let this mind be in you, which was also in Christ Jesus: Who, being in the form of God, thought it not robbery to be equal with God: But made himself of no reputation, and took upon him the form of a servant, and was made in the likeness of men: And being found in fashion as a man, he humbled himself, and became obedient unto death, even the death of the cross. Wherefore God also hath highly exalted him, and given him a name which is above every name: That at the name of Jesus every knee should bow, of things in heaven, and things in earth, and things under the earth; And that every tongue should confess that Jesus Christ is Lord, to the glory of God the Father."*

Notice, Jesus became a servant. He became obedient. He humbled Himself. What happened because of that, is He was highly exalted and given a name that is above every name. That means there is another anointing. His Name took on an anointing that it did not have before. ***God also hath highly exalted him, and given him a name which is above every name.*** That means His name before didn't carry the weight. It didn't have the yoke-destroying, burden-removing power of God until He humbled Himself, until He became obedient, until He became a servant. When He did there was an anointing that was put upon His name. There is such an anointing in the name of Jesus that every knee must bow and every tongue must confess that Jesus Christ is Lord.

There are anointings. You can tell it with some people who have healing anointings. In my life, I know tumors and growths are going to leave. Joints and bones also get healed. Those things just happen. There was a time in my life when the ears of every deaf person I ministered to popped open. I think there have been only one or two that didn't open. That is a special anointing. I remember when those things came. I remembered what happened. I know others who have special anointings for heart trouble. Almost every person they pray for who has heart problems gets healed. Or at least, a high percentage. If there is a demon anywhere, there are others who are able to spot it and cast it out. If you have any kind of attack against your mind, your thoughts, oppressions there are ministers who can spot that and drive it off. Don't ever feel ashamed because the devil is attacking you. Shame is in not allowing a person with anointing to help you. None of us have it all. That is why we have a body. Where I may excel in one area, others will excel in other area. When we all get together, we win.

Several years ago I played sports. I learned from football that if you don't have good linemen who will block for you, it doesn't make any difference how good you are at running with the ball. If the linemen are not anointed to move some weight out of the way, you are about to be splattered no matter how anointed you are to run with the football. We need one another. One person may be anointed to run with the football but you have to have some blockers, some linemen who know how to move obstacles out of the way, to move those out of the way who are coming to attack you. It takes everybody on the team to win. In the body of Christ, it is going to take everybody working together. There are anointings you can have that are so unique that they can greatly bless the body of Christ. We each have a part. No one person has all the anointing. Jesus has dispersed it throughout His body.

    Before he was anointed, Moses was in the wilderness for forty years. John the Baptist was in the wilderness before he came out anointed. The Apostle Paul spent three and a half years in the wilderness and came out with an anointing he didn't have before. When he was first converted he tried to operate in the anointing but he didn't have it. He wasn't received. The yoke of religion that was upon the people was not being destroyed. He came out of the wilderness with an anointing that shook the known world.

    Many have been through some things, fought some devils, and experienced some attacks. The way you get anointed is by coming out of it with a shout. Coming out of it knowing who God is. Coming out of it knowing who you are in God.

Approved For Ministry

We are able ministers of the New Covenant.

2 Corinthians 3:5-6; *"Not that we are sufficient of ourselves to think any thing as of ourselves; but our sufficiency is of God; Who also hath made us* [all of us, everyone who is reading this is part of "us"] *able ministers of the new testament; not of the letter, but of the spirit: for the letter killeth, but the spirit giveth life."*

You are able to do it. You have the potential to do it. Just like with the laws of inertia there is the potential and the kinetic. I am believing God to unlock the potential so that you become kinetic power in the earth. That is the job of the five-fold ministry. We minister to you so you can minister to the world. We unlock what is locked up on the inside of you that you don't even see yet. God has put it there. The five-fold ministry can spot it and unlock it so you can be released and begin to minister effectively.

There are three things that must come in order for you to minister effectively. First, you must be anointed by God. That was covered in the previous chapter. We saw how the anointing comes. Jesus, though He was destined to be the anointed one, went into a season where He actually entered into the anointing and was anointed by God. He was baptized by the Spirit before He was full of the Spirit and was called the Anointed One. Then He was led by the Spirit into the wilderness to be tempted. He came out of there and began to operate in the power of the

Spirit but was still not anointed. The anointing came after He stood in the synagogue and read the passage out of the prophet Isaiah.

Are you beginning to see how the anointing comes? You are saved and receive the infilling of the Holy Spirit when you start speaking in tongues. Then you speak in tongues enough until you are full of the Holy Ghost. Next the Holy Spirit leads you into battle, right into a confrontation with devils. But in the middle of that, you use the Word of God, press into the Word of God, press into the fullness of God and start defeating satan with the rhema, the revelation. After satan is defeated and leaves then you say, *"Now I am anointed."*

Next, Jesus was approved by God. Once God puts His stamp of approval on you signs, wonders and miracles will happen on a regular basis.

Acts 2:22; *"Ye men of Israel, hear these words; Jesus of Nazareth, a man approved of God among you by miracles and wonders and signs, which God did by him in the midst of you, as ye yourselves also know:"*

This verse is about Jesus being approved by God and what happened after He was approved. Jesus came into a place where God the Father put His stamp of approval upon Him. After this approval by God, there were miracles, wonders, and signs. First approval then signs, wonders and miracles, not an occasional faith accident like most people have. A faith accident happens when you got a miracle, don't know how you got it and don't know how to duplicate it.

Most Christians have faith accidents. They wonder what they said and how they said it. They wonder if they shouted or hollered. They are trying to figure out how to duplicate it which means they had a faith accident. This also means that they have not yet received the stamp of approval from God. Once you receive the stamp of approval from God there will be signs, wonders and miracles happening on a <u>regular</u> basis. Whenever there is one needed, it will happen. Obviously, if everybody is healed where you are ministering, you can't expect the gift of healing to operate. So, don't get disappointed if no one is healed when no one is sick. Where people need miracles, need signs, need wonders they will begin to happen if the stamp of approval has been put on your life.

There are four tests that God will take you through before you are approved and He releases signs, wonders, and miracles on a regular basis. Once you know that, you can fortify yourself and get ready to pass the tests. There is nothing worse that going into class, realizing they have scheduled a test for that day and you are not prepared. You don't know if you slept during the last class, you missed it or someone didn't tell you. It is a nightmare to come in and not be prepared for the exam. Yet, in our lives there are tests that God is constantly scheduling for us. They are not temptations. There is a difference. I am talking about God allowing certain things to happen in our lives in order to bring us to the next level. Some have not passed kindergarten and they are expecting to go to college in the spirit. It will not work. There is a progression, a growth period.

2 Corinthians 10:18; *"For not he that commendeth himself is approved, but whom the Lord commendeth."*

You can't talk God into putting the stamp of approval on you. Nor can you try to show off in front of God to get Him to look at how great you are by saying, *"You really ought to approve me."* You can't tell Him how wonderful you are, about all the awesome things you have done and expect Him to put His stamp of approval on you. He doesn't put approval on us based on that.

Commendeth means that you can't vouch for yourself and say, *"God you really should approve me for signs, wonders and miracles."* Instead, God Himself has to vouch for you before He puts the stamp of approval on you.

THE WILDERNESS TEST

Deuteronomy 8:1-2; *"All the commandments which I command thee this day shall ye observe to do, that ye may live, and multiply, and go in and possess the land which the LORD sware unto your fathers. And thou shalt remember all the way which the LORD thy God led thee these forty years in the wilderness, to humble thee, and to prove thee, to know what was in thine heart, whether thou wouldest keep his commandments, or no."*

I call this first test the wilderness test. We will all go through it. Some have already been through it, some are in it as you read this, and some are getting ready to go through it. You are in one of these three areas.

God said He took them through the wilderness to prove them, so that He could approve them. If they had passed the test then in 8 to 13 days, they could have been in the Promised Land after leaving Egypt instead of the trip taking 40 years. But they weren't ready for the exam. They hadn't passed any tests. They hadn't been through anything, hadn't fought any devils. They didn't really know what God could do.

In my own life I have fought tumors and growths on two occasions. By the power of God we defeated those things and by the mercy and grace of God received healing and deliverance. That was a wilderness. Through the power of the Lord those things were destroyed. Tumors and growth disappear in others now in my ministry.

God is ready to put a stamp of approval on you if you are successful when you come out of the wilderness.

Every Christian I have met has been through a trial, a trouble, or a hard place. God does not exempt you from life when you get saved. The Bible says it rains on the just and the unjust.[5] Ecclesiastes also says that whoever is born is full of trouble. The Word of God says that we are supposed to rejoice when someone dies and weep when they are born. When a Christian dies, their troubles are over down here. But when someone is born they are going to have to walk through some things. My grandmother used to say that Christians are so messed up and backward. We rejoice when babies are born and cry when Christians die. The book of Ecclesiastes says we are to do it the other way around.

When we begin to understand this, we will see things in a different light as humans. But, we are not just humans; we are Christians. We are now supposed to renew our mind and see things in a different light. We are not to see the troubles in our life as *"Woe is me. I pray the rapture takes place and takes me out of this mess."* We need to quit seeing things like that and see them as an opportunity to win something, get a stamp of approval and walk in a glory and a power that we never had before. It is a mindset that has to change. See your troubles as

---

[5] Matthew 5:45

an opportunity to triumph. If you will, you will get the stamp of approval. You are going to be full of trouble anyway so you might as well get something out of it. Why live your whole life full of trouble and never get anything for it? That is ridiculous. Yet there are Christians who get a little trouble and they whine and bellyache instead of walking through that thing with victory.

When you bellyache you don't get the stamp. That is one reason why it took extra long to get out of the wilderness. The Israelites kept complaining, grumbling. Every time they grumbled God would add another lap around the mountain. They weren't getting the stamp of approval. They weren't passing the wilderness test. In the wilderness you have got to be a continual praiser instead of a chronic complainer if you want to win.

Start praising God because He is God. You don't praise God for your trouble, but you praise God because He is God in the midst of it and He is going going to bring you out of it. There is an end to it. It shall come to pass. It won't stay forever. The things I faced last year, I am not facing right now. Some things I faced two weeks or a month ago I am not facing right now. Things change all the time.

Any heartache or heartbreak you might be having right now won't last forever. The devil tries to tell you it will. He tries to tell you your troubles are going to linger forever. Things are always changing and you will always move from point A to point B. Go ahead and believe God. You are going to come out of where you are at right now. If you can trust God in the midst of it, love on Him, and praise Him in the midst of your fiery furnace, the fire won't be able to burn you. You will walk out of that thing without even the smell of smoke. You can't stay in the fire forever. What was so awesome is that Jesus showed up in the middle of it. Why? Because the three young men were praising Him. They could have gotten in the middle of that fire, started complaining and got burned up. Instead they got in there and started praising the Lord.[6] They saw it in a different light. They saw it as an opportunity to get a stamp of approval on their lives. You can win this thing. Hang in there and believe God. It will change. It won't last forever. You will come out with something you didn't have before, something greater.

I hope this is encouraging you. If you are human it should. If you are one of those who float up to heaven and then come back down, never face a trial or a test, never fight a demon, never have an ache or a pain, never have someone say something awful about you or accuse you then you will not understand this teaching. But for the rest of us, it fits.

THE HERESY TEST

The second test is very unusual. I call it the heresy test.

1 Corinthians 11:18-19; *"For first of all, when ye come together in the church, I hear that there be divisions among you; and I partly believe it. For there must be also heresies among you, that they which are approved may be made manifest among you."*

When I first read that I thought it was a strange verse. Paul was saying that there really needs to be a contrast, a darkness so that you can see how bright the light is.

---

[6] Daniel 3:19-27

A heresy is a false doctrine. Paul said there must be heresies that arise so that those who are approved might be manifested. In other words, the light will always manifest.

John 1:4; *"In him was life; and the life was the light of men."*

Light produces life. Darkness and heresy do not produce life. It is very important that we are people of truth, that we are people of life and that we are people of light. If you walk in the light as He is in the light you will have fellowship one with another and the blood of Jesus Christ will cleanse you from all sin. (1 John 1:7)

If you will continue to walk in the truth and the light of the Word you will know that you are in the fullness of God and light because it will manifest. It will come to pass. God's hand will be upon it. The fullness of God will come. If you are really believing God and walking with the Lord then you know that the life of God will manifest in you.

You pass the heresy test by walking in truth and light. How do you know if you are walking in truth and light? It will manifest. There will be a manifestation of God, of glory.

I believe with all my heart that if someone is walking around saying that all roads lead to heaven (a heresy that is making the rounds now) then nobody will get saved and give their heart to Jesus. So already there is no manifestation in it. Another man or woman, like yourself, is preaching there is only one way to heaven and that is through the blood of Jesus, you must accept Jesus Christ as your Lord and Savior. Guess what! That is going to manifest. Somebody is going to get saved. That is how you know it is truth. Somebody's life that is changed is the proof of the truth. The proof of the pudding is in the eating.

We have to pass the heresy test. Are you walking in truth that is manifesting in your life?

GOD'S PLAN

The Lord has something planned for us. He plans to bless us. Jeremiah says that it is His plan to prosper us, to give us a future and a hope.[7]

Ephesians 5:13; ***"But all things that are reproved are made manifest by the light: for whatsoever doth make manifest is light."***

Light always produces life. The natural light of the sun will cause photosynthesis to take place in plants. They start growing and producing. Cows eat the plants and we eat the cows. Directly or indirectly the light is blessing us. The light is producing life for us.

The natural and the spiritual parallel each other. The light of God is the revelation of His Word. When there is true revelation flowing, there will be a manifestation coming right after it. You know you have a true revelation of salvation when you get saved. That is the only way to get saved. You receive a revelation that Jesus is the way to heaven and you are lost without Him. You need Him. When you got that revelation, there was a manifestation coming right after that called salvation and you received it.

---

[7] Jeremiah 29:11

It is the same way with healing. When you begin to understand that by His stripes you have been healed, that He is the Healer, is Jehovah Rapha; when you understand that the virtue of healing is in Him and you can tap into that by faith and receive it by faith; when you understand that it is part of your covenant and get the revelation or the light on it, it won't be long until there will be a manifestation of it.

It is the same with prosperity. There is a true prosperity but it doesn't mean that I am filling my pockets all the time. There is a full prosperity, which means I am prospering spirit, soul and body. My prosperity is being used to fund the gospel around the world. I understand that I am to prosper to become a paymaster of the gospel. I am not supposed to prosper to pad my pockets. It is not a fleshly, carnal thing. God doesn't mind you having nice things but He doesn't want those things to have you. He doesn't want you to constantly have to put lots of money on you. This is not a message people like to hear but it is true.

If you will ever get your eyes on funding the gospel, blessing the ministry, blessing the work of the gospel, blessing those who are preaching the gospel, helping build churches, helping with television and radio ministries, helping get literature to other countries, reaching into the places to feed the poor, helping those who are orphans and homeless, and put your heart into that you have already switched to God's prosperity. God will begin to fund it your way. Get a revelation of that and you will begin sowing seed. You will be faithful with your tithe because your tithe is part of your covenant. If you don't tithe, you have just broke covenant with God. It is too dangerous to be outside of the covenant of God in this world that we live in. You want to make sure you are in God's covenant by continuing to give your tithes and offerings unto the Lord. You also want to go above that and begin to make some vows and plant some seed, begin to bless the kingdom of God. You can't even do that without a revelation. Otherwise you will be thinking, *"This preacher is trying to get my money. Everybody's after my money."*

I suppose the doctor is not. I suppose the lawyer is not. The grocer certainly isn't. He will give you all the groceries you want with no money. I dare you to go to your banker with a spiritual problem. I dare you to walk into the bank, want to spend time with him, ask him to pray for you then say that you have another problem and ask for some financial assistance. I dare you to expect him to take care of you financially and spiritually and never require that you pay anything back or do anything. If he does, why then, he is in it for the money. See how ridiculous that sounds, but that is what is said about ministers. It is time for us to break that mindset because it is the wrong one.

The ministry needs support. There are people who need us to pray for them, prophesy to them, get them filled with the Holy Ghost, get them saved, get them delivered, instill things in them. It takes thousands of dollars to do that and still take care of those connected to the ministry, our own families and staff. The gospel is free, even though it cost Jesus everything. The real price is in the vehicle. The vehicle of the gospel is very expensive. Pastors know that. They are trying to get buildings or equipment, pay rent, pay off a note, take care of utilities and run a ministry. It takes a lot of funds to keep it going. The church has to change its mindset and start seeing that God is going to use us to fund the gospel. I am not prospering so that I can have stuff. You can only drive so many cars because after awhile it is kind of a nuisance. You can only live in so many houses and wear so many rings. You can only wear so many watches, after awhile it is boring. Some may wish they had some of that boring. No, you just think you would because the devil tells you that you would enjoy all of that.

I remember the first car the Lord provided for me that was paid for. I thought the feeling of getting it would be the most amazing thing. It was for a couple of days. After two days I thanked the Lord for it because it was nice but it didn't get me excited any longer like I thought it would. Things will talk to you. *"If you will buy me, all your dreams will come true."* Ever had a really nice vehicle talk to you? *"Oh, you would look so good in me. People would notice you. If you just had me all your dreams would come true."* So, you get it and for a couple of days it is nice. Then someone scratches all down the side of it, something gets spilled inside, someone hits you and dents the door.

The wealth of this world is only a tool. It doesn't satisfy the longing of your heart.

I remember a prophetess who was getting ready to go into the mountains of the Philippines to people who had never heard the gospel. It was a journey of a day or so to reach them. They were going to sleep on the ground as they traveled and ministered. No hotels. She needed $4,000 for the airline tickets and called me for prayer. If she didn't purchase the tickets quickly she would not be able to get them in time. When I hung up the phone I told God I wanted to be the person to get the tickets. I didn't have a dime.

I want to prove to you it is not about money, but about heart, faith, love. If God can find somebody who will say *"yes"* He will channel huge funds through them.

I got on my knees and wept before God. I told Him I knew He could use anybody but I wanted to be the one who would write the check that would send missionaries into remote areas of the Philippines where the gospel had never been preached. I might have been selfish with that but I wanted to be the one to make the difference. How many want to stand before the Lord having done nothing, given nothing? I don't. I want to stand before my Lord and have Him say, *"Well done, good and faithful servant."* I made a vow before the Lord. If He would give me the money I would send it as quickly as He put it into my hands. I was serious. I was not playing games.

I got a phone call that night from a man I had met. He asked me to go to brunch with him at a particular restaurant his dad owned. He himself owned 23 franchises for the Lazy Boy recliner. We got our food and blessed it. He laid his checkbook on the table and asked if it would be okay for him and his wife to bless me with a check for $7,777. He wanted to put a $7,000 check into my hand but knew that I tithe on everything. God had told them to give me the $7,000 but they wanted me to use that for whatever I wanted and not for tithe so he included the tithe in the check amount. I had not been asking for money. He wrote the check, slid it across the table and in my heart I knew where $4,000 was going. It was amazing because that was the first night of a meeting that went four weeks. As soon as I sent the $4,000 off, $20,000 came in. People who had never given were writing thousand dollar checks and handing them to me in the service. God will bless you for being obedient. I didn't lose when I gave.

The Philippine people got the news of the meetings out to the surrounding area and people traveled for a couple of days to get there. A year later the prophetess and I were at a convention where we both were speaking. Several of us got together and watched a video of what had happened in those meetings. Eight thousand people had attended. Every hand went up when she asked who wanted to be saved. Every hand went up when she asked who wanted healing because there were no doctors in the mountains. She prayed a prayer. (While watching the video you could feel the presence of God.) She asked, through the interpreter, how many believed God had healed them and how many knew they had been healed. They were to check their bodies. Every hand went up. A man who was bent over with arthritis straightened up as the power of God hit him. He took off walking. I wept. I may never see those people here on earth but I know that one day when I stand before the Lord, He will show me a section of people and ask if I remember the faith step that I took when I became available to Him.

I could have done like so many do. *"I can't afford to do anything. I am so poor I can hardly pay attention."* If I do that I will never be anything and never do anything. You can take a Gideon attitude of *"who me, Lord?"* or you can understand that your name means mighty warrior. That is what Gideon's name meant and he didn't even know it. Some don't know who they are. They are looking at how life has treated them, how the devil has stolen from them, looking at what they don't have in their hand instead of what is in His hand.

Sometimes we have to break the poverty mentality that holds us down. Remember, I didn't have it to give but when I got it, I gave and God gave me extra. I could have easily put all $7,000 in several places where it was needed but I remembered what I had told the Lord. He rewarded me and it wasn't just with money. We had a revival that lasted four weeks. Lives were being changed every night. We had angels that would stand behind people and the Lord would lead me to where they were standing. There were healings, deliverances. The Lord would tell me what their ministry was and what was happening in that person's life. This didn't happen until I released the $4,000. But I first had to believe that God could give it to me.

Some don't believe that God can even get it to them and guess what – it will never happen just because they don't believe. If you can't believe to put $50 in an offering, how can you believe for $4,000? If you can't believe God to take care of a headache, how are you going to believe Him for cancer? If you don't have enough faith to take care of a toenail problem, how are you going to believe Him for something huge? We are talking about progression.

THE STUDY TEST

Until you study and know God's Word, you are not going to get a stamp of approval. You want God to do big stuff and yet are not studying His Word. You don't even know what it says. You expect some preacher to tell you everything. How are you going to fully enter anything? Preachers are supposed to be instilling in you a desire to study. Not just read but to study the Word, to dig for yourself. Yes, they are there to equip you but they are to direct you in your study. That is what is so awesome about pastors, in particular. They can begin to direct you in studies and into mindsets so you can get your mindsets changed. You start studying and thinking about it in a different light.

2 Timothy 2:15; *"Study to shew thyself approved unto God, a workman that needeth not to be ashamed, rightly dividing the word of truth."*

If I don't study, I could wrongly divide the word of truth. Reading God's Word is the start of study but it is not the end of it. I prayerfully read the Word of God until the Holy Spirit puts His finger on something in the Word and intrigues me with it. Then out come my study tools. Years ago I used the Strong's concordance, now I have a computer. I will start looking up words and cross-references. I will start looking up all the words on a particular subject because the Holy Spirit put His finger on something that intrigued me. I want to find out about it. I start digging and digging. The Holy Spirit begins to guide my studies in a particular light. Sometimes I will stop and just shout. I have wanted to dance or run. I have stood up on occasion and done a little jig because of the revelation that came out of that study.

When you study God's Word and find the truth about the Word of God by the volume of scripture then God begins to put His stamp of approval on you. God wants us to be students of the Word. It is not that hard. Just read the Word until something intrigues you or you want to know something or the Holy Ghost touches it and it jumps off the page into your heart. Then start looking up all the verses on that subject that you can find. If you don't know how to do that, find someone who does and ask them to teach you how to do that.

THE FINANCE TEST

Then there is the finance test. Before God will release His strong glory and power in your life, He will test you with money. If He cannot trust you with finances, He will not trust you with His glory.

Luke 16:10; *"He that is faithful in that which is least is faithful also in much: and he that is unjust in the least is unjust also in much."*

God knows this principle. If you can't be faithful in one area, you won't be faithful in another.

Luke 16:11; *"If therefore ye have not been faithful in the unrighteous mammon* [finances]*, who will commit to your trust the true riches?"*

The true riches are anointing, healing, glory, the power of God, the fullness of God, ministries that are effective. If He can't trust you with finances and the giving of tithes and offerings, if He can't speak to you and ask you to give a certain offering without you saying you can't do it then how can He trust you with His glory, with healing ministries, with signs, wonders and miracles? How can He trust you with something that great when you can't even handle your giving? This is the Word. This is not something Phillip Rich came out with.

Let me tell you what happens to us. We hear about a minister who took advantage of people with offerings or maybe we saw it happen. So now we throw the baby out with the bathwater. Anyone who says anything about offerings is evil so we throw everything out. Yet, it is God's Word that says that we should give. The principles are from Genesis to Revelation. Don't throw the baby out with the bathwater. Just throw out the dirty water. Throw out the practices that are not scriptural. Giving to the ministry, blessing the ministry, helping with missions, helping with the local church, helping to support ministers, helping support the work of God, helping with orphanages, helping to feed the poor are all good things and they are what God has told us to do in His Word. Just because somebody did something wrong doesn't mean you throw everything out.

I have heard of bankers who were not honest so does that mean we should never ever put money in the bank? You can't trust any banker? Isn't that stupid? Yet the devil will use that on us and twist it so that when the real men and women of God come along and challenge us to give we think they are of the devil. The Word of God tells us that we are supposed to support the work of the Lord, support the ministry.

You pass the finance test by being faithful with your tithes (10% off the top), faithful with offerings and giving whenever God tells you to give. If God speaks to your heart to give, don't tell Him "*no*." If you tell Him "*no*," He can't trust you anymore. There have been times when I have had the Lord speak to me and tell me He wanted me to do this and this. My natural head is going, "*But, Lord!*"

I heard one minister give a testimony several years ago. He needed thousands of dollars to pay for television time and to repair the building he was in. He went into prayer and asked God to meet the need, to bring the finances in. God spoke to him to give away his van. He immediately rebuked the devil, like most of us would. Here he was praying for finances and a voice comes telling him to give his van away. He got up from prayer and quit praying. He got on an airplane, started thinking again about all the money he needed and began to pray again. This time he began to understand that God was talking to him. He heard God say that he was to give away his van and seven of his suits. He got upset and said, "*God, earlier you said you wanted me to give my van away. Now you want me to give the van and seven suits. What is with this God? I am the one with the need.*" The Lord answered, "*I know it. I am trying to meet this thing for you but you have to put your seed in my hands. You are not willing to do that so I have nothing to work with."* He finally realized that if he didn't hear God this time, the next time it might be the boat, the television, the seven suits and the van.

    I have had God increase my giving when I wouldn't listen to Him. There was one time I heard the Lord tell me to give a certain amount of money. I messed around and ended up giving a couple hundred of dollars above that. My wife asked me why I wrestled so much with it because I ended up having to give more. The end result of the story is that this minister gave those things away and God began to speak to other people.

    There are Boazes all around you watching your life. There are people who know you who have the means to bless you beyond your wildest dreams. But God isn't going to talk to them until you get into covenant with God, until you pass the finance test, until you start giving your tithes and offerings, until you start obeying God. Until you do, God will never speak to the Boazes to do anything for you.

    So, here I was positioning myself with the $4,000 vow. I didn't know that guy made $15 million a year. I was prophesying to him and his wife about how the prophetic was in their life, how their whole life was prophetic. They already knew that. Bill Hamond had prophesied it to them two weeks before. It was the same prophecy. They were Methodists looking for a full gospel prophetic church. I was in that church for four weeks. At the end of that time, they had found a church. They even bought the church a new building and fixed it up. The old building would seat 120, the new one 400.

Are you ready to pass some tests and see the hand of God come upon your life with His stamp of approval with signs, wonders and miracles on a regular basis? God is just looking for somebody to qualify. Benny Hinn, Oral Roberts, Kathryn Kuhlman passed the tests and qualified to enter their ministries. They got the approval and things happened in their ministry. God is waiting for you to pass some tests so He can put the stamp of approval on you.

Appointed For Ministry

2 Timothy 1:11; *"Whereunto I am appointed a preacher, and an apostle, and a teacher of the Gentiles."*

The root word of *"appointed"* means to be set in a position, to be ordained or to be sent. You have heard of people who weren't sent but they just packed up and went. They had some anointing on them so they assumed. Presumption is a sin. God didn't really say it but they presumed it because of some criteria that they had set up. *"Last week I prayed for somebody and they got healed. Now I presume God wants me to quit my job, go on the road and prayer for those who are sick. I haven't been approved yet and haven't been appointed."*

I have been called to be a prophet to the nations all my life. I was called from my mother's womb to be a missionary. Missionary and apostle are almost the same term. I tried on several occasions and assumed that I had the appointment. I would try to jump out, do it and the door would slam on me because I didn't have an appointment. I had somewhat of an anointing but I had a self-appointment spirit.

A couple of years ago the Lord opened Mexico to me by connecting me with Apostle Fred Pine. He invited me to go there with him. Having been there seventeen or eighteen years at that time, he knew the ropes and could train me. God did not want to just thrust me in blindly but to put me with seasoned people who knew the ropes so that I could be trained and do it right, and acquire some wisdom. I wouldn't get in there, make a lot of mistakes and hurt a lot of people before I finally learned what I was doing.

I went into Mexico not trying to do it my way, change Apostle Pine, or change what they did. I just went with the flow. I began to share with Apostle Pine what my vision of missions was. He had the same vision inside of him and together we have been able to implement it. We began to work together and there were all kinds of miracles and healings. A crippled woman got out of a wheelchair and walked. Two hundred people had tumors disappear. Homosexuals who were pastoring churches came to Apostle Pine and weeping said they didn't want that life style anymore. They wanted prayer and deliverance. People were running up and grabbing Apostle Pine's hands to place them on tumors. Tumors disintegrated when his hands barely touched them. A year and a half later we were still hearing testimonies from that trip.

God spoke to me and said, *"Now I am going to send you to the nations."* That meant my appointment. Remember, I had been called as a little boy. I have seen the faces of the nations all my life. In the crusades in Mexico I saw masses of people being saved, healed, set free. The crippled are walking, miracles are happening. I have seen all of this in dreams and visions all my life. But just in the last year has God said that now He will send me to the nations.

Apostle Pine was sitting next me at a conference and he turned to me to say, *"God is opening missions to you. You will be going into all the world. There will be invitations for you to go where other missionaries cannot go. They are going to ask you to go in their place."* The next day Jeff Johns, pastor of Whitehorse Christian Center, told me he was scheduled to go to Bangladesh and Cambodia but couldn't. Would I go in his place? This was a fulfillment of a prophecy that was given twenty-four hours earlier. As he was asking, Jeff Johns disappeared and I saw Jesus sitting in his chair. Jesus asked me to go to Bangladesh and Cambodia for Him. When God appoints you, doors open supernaturally. If doors are not opening it means the appointment is not yet. There is a season for it. There are some things for you to fulfill.

The Lord took me through some hard places, some wilderness experiences to get me anointed. I needed to pass some tests and be approved. He also wanted to prepare me because now the School of the Prophets, all four years, has been developed. The School consists of four years of intense teaching about the prophetic, developing people in the prophetic. The Lord set me aside to develop the teaching on the prophetic: manuals, teachings, tape series.[8] All of this material will go to the nations. God wanted to develop me and prepare me before He appointed me.

W. B. Grant, Sr. was a powerful man of God and a man of integrity. I did not get to know him personally but through his writings. When he was a new Christian he went to some meetings. A prophetess called him out and told him he was called to the nations. Signs, wonders and miracles were going to happen. He went home and packed his bag. As he was headed out the door his uncle asked him where he was going. *"I got this prophecy that I am going to go to the nations and have signs, wonders and miracles."* His uncle asked if he had heard that from God. No, he had heard it from a prophetess. His uncle answered, *"Well, you had better stop by, pick her up and take her with you because you can't hear God for yourself."* He went back to his room and threw his bag on the bed.

---

[8] For more information on how you can take the School of the Prophets course, contact us online at epaministries.com or call 765-420-7885.

He began to pray two hours a day and to ask the Lord what He wanted him to do. The Lord told him He wanted him to go into business. The Lord told him about a piece of property he was to buy. It was a car lot so he began to sell cars and started prospering. He still prayed two hours a day seeking the will of God for his life. The Lord told him to buy the grocery store next door. He did. Over the next years he bought more businesses and after about ten years had put back $300,000 in savings. Then the Lord told him to sell everything he had, go to the mission fields and pray for the sick. The appointment came. The money he had funded him for the first few years until the support began to kick in.

Some are sent. Others just packed up and went. I can tell you it is discouraging when you are called and are chomping at the bit wanting to go out there and do it. But when you do that you will fail, fall, hit snags and be so discouraged that you will wonder if you ever were called. You will want to quit all together. God doesn't want you to do that. The best thing you can do is to be faithful in the local church. Be there on time, pay your tithes, give your offerings, pray, be involved, and put your hand to something. Do that on a regular basis faithfully. Then the day will come when God will speak. It will be so loud you will not miss it. God will speak to you and say, "*Now!*"

This is very practical. Being spiritual doesn't means you have to be flighty or stupid. Being spiritual doesn't mean you need to be granola – a nut, a fruit or a flake. Being spiritual doesn't mean you are a space cadet. You don't have to act weird all the time.

FIVE DISCIPLINES

To be spiritual means to be down to earth and real, to live right, to treat people right, to share the love of Christ, to develop the five spiritual disciplines. Those disciplines are the reading of the Word daily, prayer daily, witnessing, giving tithes and offerings faithfully and hooking up with a local church.

Witnessing means you live a life style of witnessing. Let your light so shine before men. That means you can't start talking about Jesus, then turn around and cuss somebody out. You can't talk about Jesus, turn around and talk about getting drunk. Let your light shine and then open your mouth. You have no right to open your mouth if you are not living it. Otherwise you will hurt the witness and the testimony of Jesus. Live it and then open your mouth as God directs.

There is a time to shut your mouth and walk it particularly with family. They already know where you stand. You can get too preachy with them and turn them off. A life style will really get them as they see you serve the Lord, love the Lord, are faithful to go to the house of God, faithful in your tithes and offerings, and faithful to live for the Lord. They will see all of that and it will speak volumes to them about who Jesus really is and that He is real.

Giving tithes and offerings means you live a lifestyle of being a generous giver. Don't miss a paycheck where you take ten percent out and give it to the Lord. Don't let it slide and say you will do it the next time. What you are doing is not being faithful. You will miss your appointment.

Hook up with a local church, become a member, become a part and be faithful to attend.

These are five disciplines that every Christian must develop in their life. If you do, you will get your appointment in due season.

ARE YOU SENT?

2 Timothy 1:11; *"Whereunto I am appointed a preacher, and an apostle, and a teacher of the Gentiles."*

Paul said that he was appointed as a preacher, apostle and teacher. His appointment was to the Gentiles. It was also connected to a place and a people.

Part of my appointment has been to selected parts of the country, to places I go on a regular basis. God has appointed me to the people there. These people love me and I love them. There is covenant relationship. I can't just go and preach anywhere that God hasn't sent me. I get invitations that I don't take. Why? They are not my appointment. I would be stepping out of my appointment if God hasn't sent me. The sending is the appointment. I can't just go anywhere. I go where He sends me. I am sent to a people. When I am in Mexico – I am sent to a people. When I went to Bangladesh and Cambodia, I was sent to a people, appointed to go there. I had success.

Wherever you are appointed, God gives you a people. I heard the Lord speak to me, *"Phil, I have given you a people."* What did He mean by that? They will accept me. There is a people who will hear what I have to say and they will connect with the Spirit of God that is within me. They will understand me. They will hear me. It will make sense to them when it wouldn't to somebody else. I have heard people tell me I teach so simple and right on that they can understand it. That is because I was appointed to them. Someone else could come from another place who had not been appointed, try to fit in and the teaching not make a bit of sense to the listeners. It is a people that we are sent to. Don't be discouraged if God doesn't send you to everybody. He will send you to a people. Wherever He sends you, that is where your appointment is. That is what you have to accept.

Matthew 10:5-6; *"These twelve Jesus sent forth [appointed], and commanded them, saying, Go not into the way of the Gentiles, and into any city of the Samaritans enter ye not: But go rather to the lost sheep of the house of Israel."*

Jesus was sending them into a specific place. He was appointing them to a place. Your appointment is to somebody. You already have an appointment to your family: in-laws, spouses, children, grandchildren. You may not like your appointment but you have it. If you will be faithful to that appointment, walk the line and live the life, God will open up another appointment. The Lord said that whoever is faithful over the little things, He would make a ruler over the many. (Matthew 5:23) Many cannot be faithful with what they have. Yet they are dreaming of great things for God.

I heard a lady minister say that there are people who want to take authority over all the principalities and power over the cities and yet cannot take authority over a sink full of dirty dishes. See how practical that is.

You are appointed to a place or a position. You are appointed to a people. You are also appointed for a purpose.

Paul is speaking to King Agrippa in the following verses.

Acts 26:15-18; *"And I said, Who art thou, Lord? And he said, I am Jesus whom thou persecutest. But rise, and stand upon thy feet: for I have appeared unto thee for this purpose, to make thee a minister and a witness both of these things which thou hast seen, and of those things in the which I will appear unto thee; Delivering thee from the people, and from the Gentiles, unto whom now I send thee, To open their eyes, and to turn them from darkness to light, and from the power of Satan unto God, that they may receive forgiveness of sins, and inheritance among them which are sanctified by faith that is in me."*

Paul received an appointment. The purpose of the appointment was to open the eyes of the people, to turn them from darkness to light, from the power of satan to God that they might receive forgiveness and an inheritance. Every appointment has a purpose. You have to find out what the purpose of your appointment is. For me a lot of the purpose for my appointments has been to teach and instill the correct prophetic flow in the church. In some places it is for me to be prophetic. In other places it may be to be apostolic and to set in order, to enhance, to set on the right track, to set souls on fire so that people will be doing what they are supposed to be doing for the Lord.

You also have to hear God about what church you are supposed to be a part of. You are not just to go to any church. You have heard people say to go to the church of your choice. Wrong! You don't have any say in it. You go to the church of His choice. He chooses where you go.

He will not send you to a demon-infested church because you don't have the power to change that pastor and all the people. I have seen so many people who felt they were called to go in and change a pastor. That is out of order. The only one who can change a pastor ultimately is God. But God will use another pastor or an apostolic prophetic ministry that is over that ministry to set them in order. If no one is there to do it, don't waste your time, your money or your effort. Get out of that place while you can before you come under attack.

Be where you are supposed to be. If God appoints you to a church, go to that church. Your purpose there is to hook up with the vision of that church. Don't try to implement your own vision. Set your vision on a shelf and find out what the vision is of the pastor is. The vision should be available. The Bible says to write the vision and make it plain so we can run with it.[9] Read the vision or set up an appointment to meet with the Pastor so he can share the vision with you. Then pray and ask God to help you take that vision and be a part of it. Work within the boundaries of it. Do not try to put your vision there and make it work. Did you know that two visions bring division? If your vision is of God then later God will show a place for that vision to come into play. The Pastor may come to you and say he has an area in his ministry that he needs someone to come in and work. You may end up thinking, *"That is my vision."* And you get an appointment.

Sometimes appointments will come by invitation from other anointed people of God. When Apostle Pine asked me to go to Mexico with him, that was an appointment. When Jeff Johns asked me to take his place and go to Bangladesh and Cambodia, that was an appointment. With an appointment

---
[9] Habakkuk 2:2

finances will also come. Every time God has called me to Mexico, He has caused the finances to come in before I went. You must make sure you wait for your appointment because with the appointment will come the provision. God will always pay for what He orders. If you order it, you will pay for it and we do not have enough money for that.

AN APPOINTED TIME

There is an appointed time.

Galatians 4:1-2; *"Now I say, That the heir, as long as he is a child, differeth nothing from a servant, though he be lord of all; But is under tutors and governors until the time appointed of the father."*

Galatians 4:4; *"But when the fulness of the time was come, God sent forth his Son, made of a woman, made under the law,"*

When the fullness of time has come God will send you, that means He will appoint you when the time is right, when you have passed the test and prepared yourself, developed the five disciplines, have been a part of the body of Christ, and have learned to bloom where you are planted. Plant yourself in the house of the Lord and you will flourish and bring forth fruit.[10] God will do nothing outside of His body and outside of His church so you might as well be a part of it. Quit running from it. Quit running out and trying to do your own thing. It takes time to develop. Wait for your appointment. Otherwise you will get out from under your covering The devil will tempt

---

[10] Psalms 92:10-14

you, you will not have money, will not have support, nobody praying for you, nobody backing you, a lone ranger floundering all by yourself about to drown, the wolves are chasing after you nipping at your heels, all your life is falling apart and you are saying, "*God, why is this happening to me?*" The reason I can preach this so well is because I have done it and I don't ever want to do it again. I have learned my lesson. I have learned that is not the way to go. I am not going that way again. I am smart enough to know not to do that.

If you can learn from my experience then you don't have to go through what I went through. I almost lost my marriage doing that. I was called but I wasn't waiting for an appointment. I was jumping out of the boat with no backing, no finances, no church connected to it. I had no apostolic covering. I was out on my own. I thought that was how you did it. Just me and Jesus doing our own thing. I found out Jesus does not work with that. He has a body. If you are connected to the body and are a part of the body by hooking up with the local church, having pastors, having five-old ministry, having people over you to train you, to love you, to equip you, to pray for you, having brothers and sisters who love and support you, you love them and they love you then at that point God will bring an appointment. With the appointment will come the provision and the protection.

A COVERING

There is a time and a season for everything. All things will be made beautiful in His time.[11] I may be ready to preach now. I may be ready to evangelize the world. I may be

---

[11] Ecclesiastes 3:1,11

ready to jump out on my own and do it. It doesn't mean He is ready for me or that He has appointed me. Just because I am anointed doesn't mean I am appointed. I was anointed long before I was appointed. Twenty years ago I was anointed. I prayed for people who were deaf and nine out of ten were healed of any kind of deafness. I thought that meant I could go to the nations. I was anointed but I wasn't approved yet. I hadn't passed any tests. I assumed that because I was so anointed I was also appointed.

The appointment comes later. It comes through faithfulness, walking it out with the Lord, being obedient to the Lord, being accountable to someone other than myself. We think our accountability stops with us. We need to be accountable to God's people, to God's leaders. Before I make big decisions I call my apostolic daddy. I will bounce it off of him. Sometimes he will have a word for me, sometimes a word of wisdom, sometimes a word of agreement. Even if I already knew it was the Lord, I need to hear his covering voice say to me, *"That's God, brother. You have heard the Lord and my blessing rests upon you."* There is a father's blessing that comes through the apostolic fathers, the Daddies.

Part of your appointment cannot be fulfilled without the correct spiritual covering over you. I am not talking about controlling spirits. God doesn't want anyone to control your life but Him. But He definitely wants a covering over you. Apostle Pine carries an umbrella of authority all over him. He can walk into a room and devils start moving out of there. He got it from his spiritual daddy who was an apostle, who got it from his spiritual daddy who was an apostle and so on up the line. Because I am under his covering, I feel what he feels now. As soon as I connected with Apostle Pine other pastors started coming to me asking me to be their apostle. That had never happened before. That covering blessing helped me to receive an appointment.

Remember, I was destined to be an apostle and a prophet all of my life. I heard God say that He had called me to be an apostle and a prophet. The apostle part didn't really kick in until I came under an apostle. My apostolic father does not control my life. He does not tell me everything to do in my life. He doesn't bark out commands and expect me to follow them. This is a man who loves me, prays for me. I can call for prayer anytime. He speaks the Word of God over me and corrects me with tears.

One time when we were in a service and I was preaching and the preaching was supernatural and the revelation was thick. I was listening to myself and saying, *"This is not me."* The message was challenging people. When I was finished I knew I should quit but the people were pulling on me and I began to prophecy to them. I messed up and I knew it. After the meeting, Apostle Pine took me aside and asked me why I had done that. I answered because the people were drawing on me. He knew that but also knew I had them going the right way and prepared for the service the next evening. I knew they had been drawing on me but I had taken away from what God had done because I ministered as the people wanted me to instead of the way God wanted it. He said all of that to me with tears. He told me never to do that again. I received what he said and told him that with God's help I would never do that again. I was sorry.

Any man who thinks he is beyond failure will say, *"Bless God, I am a man of God. He had not better talk to me like that."* That attitude will already flunk you out of the anointing. You have messed up your appointment and you are in trouble with God. Before honor comes humility. Humility means submission to authority. If you submit to nobody you are full of pride. If there is not a preacher good enough for you to submit to, a minister without enough integrity then you are already in pride. Submission is humility.

Don't let anybody correct you, just those who are in covenant with you. When my kids were growing up I didn't let everybody in the neighborhood spank my children.
Make sure you are in covenant with those who correct you. And make sure that with this covenant they are a spiritual daddy and a spiritual momma.

Made in the USA
Middletown, DE
02 September 2022